DIY AND TRANSFORM YOUR PIANO INTO A BEAUTIFUL SHELL TO HOLD A DIGITAL, WEIGHTED KEYBOARD

Gen Z Pianos

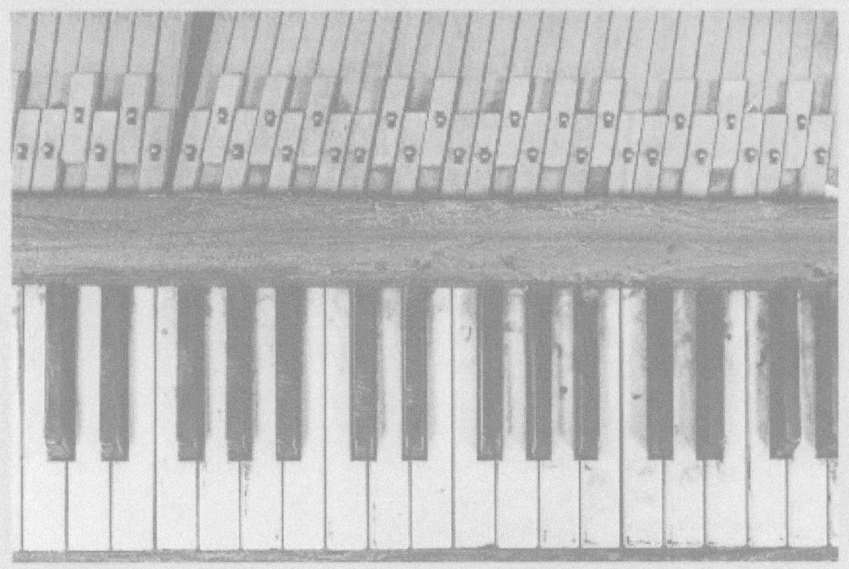

Copyright © 2020 by LK Dominguez and Reader's Select.
All rights reserved. No part of the illustrations or original work of the author may be reproduced. The authors/publishers take no responsibility for injuries or failures. Reader's Select recommends that only those who are accomplished with power tools take on this project. Remember that this is a guide based on experience and pianos are different but similar. The writer believes that all pianos can be converted into digital shells. Reader's select may recommend certain brands but takes no responsibility for the warranties or qualifications of those brands.

Phrases from public domain works are not copyrighted.

Published by Reader's Select

www.ebookwriter.net

Does your piano look like this?

Or this?

Do you have a lovely piano that just isn't perfect and you or a family member wants to play beautiful music but the piano is just holding you back?

Yes, you can replace butt springs and hammers, but have you tried taking everything out of a piano and then putting it back together? More oft than not you will end up having another problem.

And yet, the piano is so beautiful! Okay, so we can refinish your piano and remove enough to create a shell for a digital insert. Or, you can do it yourself!

This is a guide to help you.

tools

- an upright piano
- measuring tape
- electric screwdriver
- black felt to create a keyboard cover and attach to surfaces that hold your new digital insert!
- skill saw
- Needle nose pliers/cutter
- Ziploc bag for the screws
- travel, weighted keyboard that measures a few inches shorter than the front of your piano. Measure! https://amzn.to/36pp36t
- A piano tuner Wrench https://amzn.to/39GXWpC
- pedals if you want them, but most digital pianos do come with the suspension pedal https://amzn.to/36rjYuq

lift the top of the piano and remove keyboard cover

- pop loose the keys from the long wires that attach them to the hammer rail
- You have to remove the large hammer rail by unscrewing very large screws from the side of the piano. They attach to the frame
- Lift out the hammer rail
- Pop out the loosened keys (keep them to make a neat wall hanging later)

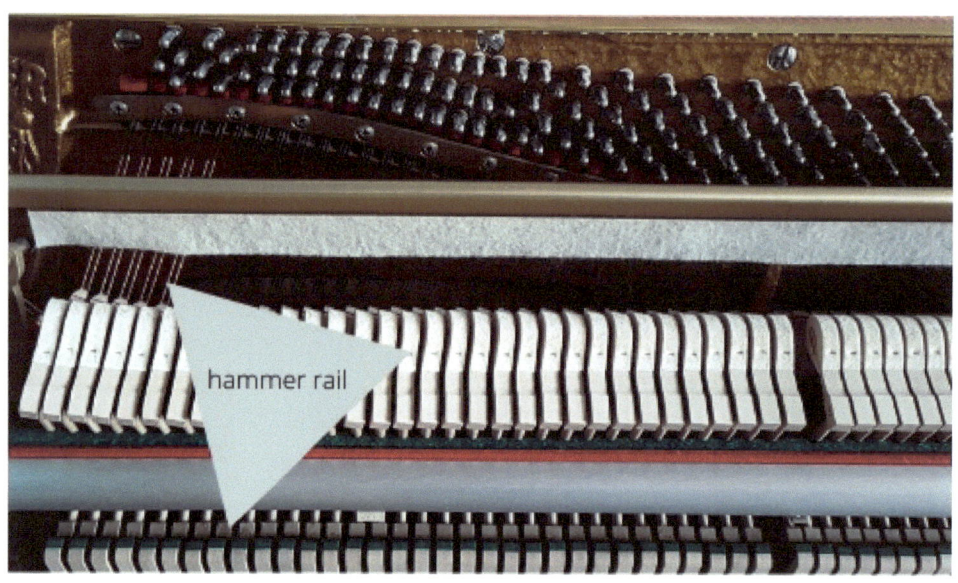

lift out the hammer rail after unscrewing it from metal plate

another picture of how the hammer rail is attached

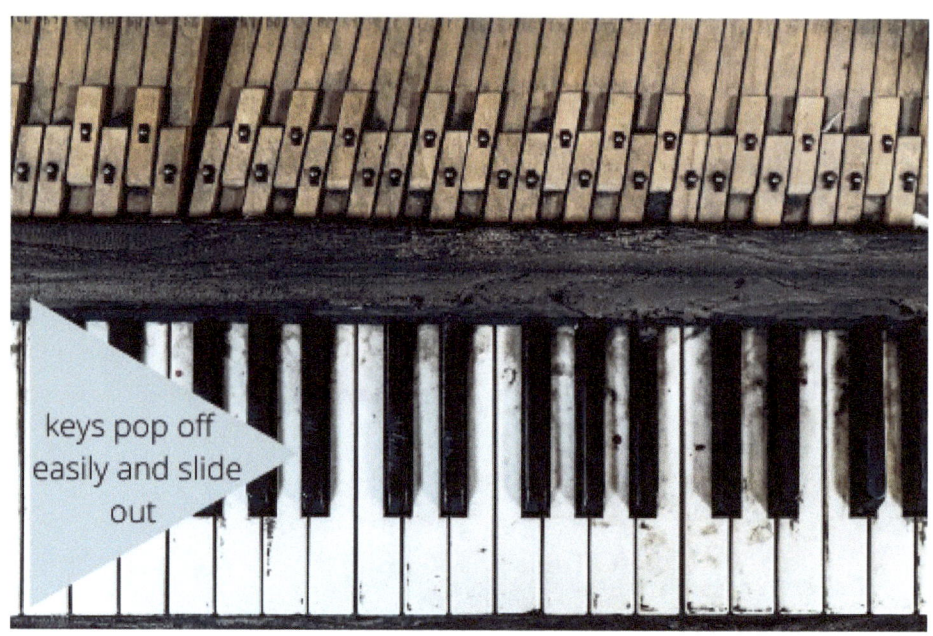

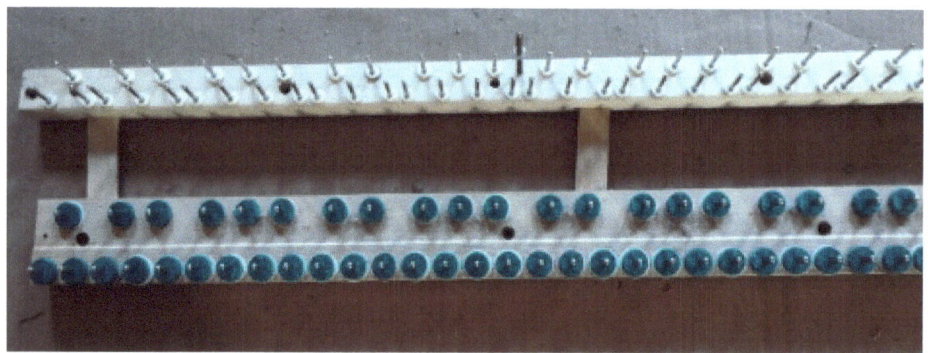

This entire piece must be removed. The keys fit on it. You can save it to arrange your keys into a wall hanging.

unscrew hammer rail from cast iron plate

Loosen all the strings

- Use the Piano Wrench to loosen all the strings. You have to do this! The strings have so much tension and you can get injured if you try cutting tense strings.
- Loosen the strings and then cut them. Yes, you can leave them and weave long strips of felt to silence them. Your choice.
- Either turn strings to loosen them entirely and then pull out strings with needle nose and leave piano pins or pull out the pins with the drill (we use the drill/electric screwdriver to unscrew them)

You can remove the iron plate or leave it to give your piano a sturdy frame. Notice the removed pins.

unscrew everything and detach pedals

take pictures and keep screws to reuse

Cut and screw in even pieces with skill saw to hold the keyboard. Use wood from inside the piano! Connect above the legs. You may have to use your ingenuity if your piano doesn't look like this! Use felt to create a nice ledge.

Turn your piano into a shell that will hold a digital insert. Look for just the weighted keyboard of your choice, but measure to make sure it will fit.

Piano needs to sit above this screw, which is attached to the leg

Use pieces from the piano to recreate a structure that will hold your digital, weighted keyboard

remove the pedals

Attach a support beam here (not shown) if you want to attach the pedals

After fitting the keyboard, sand and paint your piano shell.

notice the piano drops lower, which is why we created the side ledges. You can put a full board under the piano but it could change the piano sound.

Sand and paint your bench. Reattach necessary parts of the piano. The keyboard cover might not fit but you can buy a felt cover for your keyboard

add a lip to hold music

reinforce the wood behind the pedals with a beam of "left over wood" then replace this board. You can attach the pedals to the front or wire the sustaining pedal through the pedal holes.

return this front piece of wood to create a finished look

Extras

- Sell your extra parts on E bay!
- Don't expect this project to be easy, it's a custom project
- Remember that this is a guide! Study your digital piano insert before buying to see how you can get it to fit.
- Use felt and be careful not to scratch your insert.
- Take your time.
- Make sure to adjust/create places for your chords to hide
- Don't glue/permanently attach your piano, especially if you need to move. Save the box and you can easily box the digital piano for travel and move your piano frame separately.

We hope that our project will help yours! Be safe and take your time. Remember to measure.

www.ingramcontent.com/pod-product-compliance
Lightning Source LLC
Chambersburg PA
CBHW041542040426
42446CB00002B/199